The Weather Tracker's Handbook

Gregory C. Aaron

RUNNING PRESS

PHILADELPHIA • LONDON

9
Digit on the right indicates the number of this printing.
Library of Congress Cataloging-in-Publication Number 90–53676
ISBN 0–89471–998–X

Picture researcher: Gillian Speeth
Book interior design by Robert Perry
Certified consulting meteorologist: Lowell Krawitz, Ph.D.
Package and book cover design by Toby Schmidt
Package front and back illustrations by Bob Walters
Package back photographs:left side, top to bottom: Official U.S Navy photograph PH3 by B.A. Richards; Courtesy of NOAA/NESDIS, National Center for Atmospheric Research/National Science Foundation. Right side: National Center for Atmospheric Research/National Science Foundation.
Package interior photograph: © L. Marshall/FPG International
Additional package photographs by Bel-Hop Studios
Book cover photograph: Photo Researchers/Science Source: © Kent Wood
Book interior photographs: Courtesy of G.E.: p. 59. Grant Heilman: pp. 10, 11 (top), 9, 24, 27 (middle), 35, 36, 64, 70, 72; Larry Lefever from Grant Heilman: pp. 6, 51 (left); Runk/Schoenberger from Grant Heilman: p. 18; Alan Pitcairn from Grant Heilman: p. 50 (bottom); Hal Harrison from Grant Heilman: p. 74. © K. Martensen/Greenpeace: p. 31. Hulton/Bettmann: p. 46. National Center for Atmospheric Research/National Science Foundation: pp. 27, 32, 33, 34, 41, 58. Courtesy of NOAA/NESDIS: p. 47. Courtesy of NOAA: p. 15. Photo Researchers: © Jack Fields, pp.7, 23; © Myron Wood, p. 27 (top); OSC © Steve Krasemann, pp. 50 (top), 57; © Lawrence Migdale, p. 63. Photo Researchers/The National Audubon Siciety Collection: © Tom Hollyman, p. 11 (bottom); © Keith Gunnar, p. 20. Photo Researchers/Science Source: © Jerry Schad, p. 51 (right). UPI/Bettmann: pp. 14, 45, 75. Official U.S. Navy photograph: pp. 44, 46..
Book interior illustrations by Christine Coligan

Typography by Commcor Communications Corporation, Philadelphia, Pennsylvania

This book may be ordered by mail from the publisher.
Please add $2.50 for postage and handling.
But try your bookstore first!

Running Press Book Publishers
125 South Twenty-second Street
Philadelphia, Pennsylvania 19103–4399

A Note to Parents and Children:

This interactive, educational kit is designed to teach and entertain children, but it contains small objects which could cause injury, including severe injury if swallowed. This kit should not be used by children younger than eight years of age without adult supervision.

The first rule of weather tracking is to *respect the weather*. Stay indoors before and during a thunderstorm, hurricane, hailstorm, and other dangerous conditions.

Please read the complete instructions inside before using this kit.

—Running Press Book Publishers

CONTENTS

PART ONE

The Weather Machine

Weather is the greatest show on earth. It produces the most exciting and beautiful events we see: lightning, snowflakes, rainbows, and warm, sunny days. And nothing is more important in our daily lives than the weather. It affects the food farmers grow, our choice of clothing, and it can even change our travel plans.

Because the weather is so important, the ability to predict it is one of the most fascinating and useful skills you can have. Scientists who study the weather are called *meteorologists* (me-tee-or-AHL-uh-jists). It's their job to forecast how the weather will change from day to day. While meteorologists can usually make accurate predictions, the weather always holds surprises.

This book and kit will reveal some of the weather's secrets to you. First you'll read about the forces that work in the sky, and the terms meteorologists use. Then you'll learn to set up your own weather station. As an amateur meteorologist, you'll be able to record current conditions and predict future weather.

As warm air rises, it creates perfect winds for a balloon race.

What's the Weather?

Weather is the general condition of the blanket of air (called the *atmosphere*) above us. As you read this, the weather outside your home might be rainy or sunny, foggy or smoggy, warm or cold.

The typical weather in an area is called that area's *climate*. The most important things to know about a climate are its average seasonal temperatures and the amount of rain and snow that the area receives during the year. For instance, Oregon has moderate temperatures and receives a lot of rain throughout the year. Even though Oregon has some sunny days, we say its climate is rainy. The air in Antarctica is almost always cold and dry, so we say that Antarctica has a cold or polar climate. How would you describe the climate in your area?

When water evaporates off your skin, you feel cooler.

By studying rocks, fossils, and other evidence, scientists have discovered that the climate of the earth changes over long periods of time. For reasons that are not well understood, the earth sometimes grows warmer or colder. About 18,000 years ago, the earth was in an "ice age." At that time, average temperatures were 10° F (6° C) lower than they are now. This caused huge sheets of ice, up to a mile thick, to grow and cover large areas of land. If you live in the northern United States, Canada, or in a mountain area, your neighborhood was probably frozen solid during this ice age.

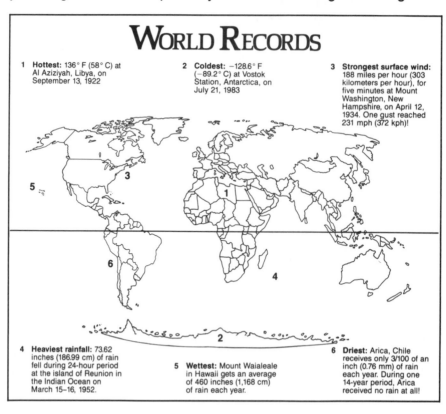

WORLD RECORDS

1 **Hottest:** 136° F (58° C) at Al Aziziyah, Libya, on September 13, 1922

2 **Coldest:** −128.6° F (−89.2° C) at Vostok Station, Antarctica, on July 21, 1983

3 **Strongest surface wind:** 188 miles per hour (303 kilometers per hour), for five minutes at Mount Washington, New Hampshire, on April 12, 1934. One gust reached 231 mph (372 kph)!

4 **Heaviest rainfall:** 73.62 inches (186.99 cm) of rain fell during 24-hour period at the island of Reunion in the Indian Ocean on March 15–16, 1952.

5 **Wettest:** Mount Waialeale in Hawaii gets an average of 460 inches (1,168 cm) of rain each year.

6 **Driest:** Arica, Chile receives only 3/100 of an inch (0.76 mm) of rain each year. During one 14-year period, Arica received no rain at all!

An Ocean of Air

The air above us is a giant weather machine, and the sun is the engine that makes it run. The atmosphere stretches hundreds of miles up from the ground and becomes thinner as it extends into space. The atmosphere has five layers, each with its own unique features.

THE TROPOSPHERE

The Greek word *tropos* means "turning" or "mixing." The troposphere is constantly in motion, and it's in this layer that most change in weather occurs. The troposphere extends from the ground to a height of about 5.5 miles (8.8 kilometers) over the poles, and about 10 miles (16 km) over the equator.

Glaciers once covered portions of the Rocky Mountains.

Spring blossoms

Summer corn

Fall harvest

Winter icicles

Although it is not very deep, the troposphere contains about four-fifths of the gas that blankets the earth. Most of the troposphere is made of nitrogen, followed by oxygen, argon, carbon dioxide, and small amounts of other gases. The troposphere also contains dust, salt (from the oceans), pollen, pollutants from cars and factories, and water vapor. The higher you go in the troposphere, the colder it gets; the top is a chilling 60° F below zero (−51° C).

THE STRATOSPHERE

The stratosphere stretches from the top of the troposphere to a height of about 30 miles (48 km). *Stratos* means "layer," and the stratosphere is usually one calm layer of thin air. Jet pilots like the stratosphere because the calm air allows them to travel at top speeds.

In the upper reaches of the stratosphere, the temperature can be even warmer than on the earth's surface. This is because a gas called *ozone*, a form of oxygen, absorbs ultraviolet radiation from the sun. In small amounts, ultraviolet radiation gives us suntans. But in larger doses, it can cause skin cancer and kill plants. Pollutants from aerosol cans, air conditioners, and factories are slowly destroying the ozone layer in the stratosphere. Many countries are now trying to limit the use of ozone-destroying chemicals.

THE MESOSPHERE

The layer of air from 30 to 50 miles (48 to 80 km) above the earth, the mesosphere is very thin and cold, with temperatures dropping to −150° F (−100° C). But there is enough air in the mesosphere to get in the way of satellites and meteors. As they fall through the mesosphere, these objects collide with billions of gas particles. This creates heat, which usually burns up the falling objects long before they hit the ground. Every day, millions of meteors burn up as they pass through the mesosphere.

THE THERMOSPHERE

Thermo is Greek for heat. The thermosphere, which extends from 50 to more than 300 miles (80 to 480 km) above the earth, is constantly bombarded with large amounts of radiation. The radiation causes the scattered air particles in this layer to become electrically charged. Radio waves bounce off the charged particles and can be received beyond the horizon.

THE EXOSPHERE

At this layer, the atmosphere blends into the

THE ATMOSPHERE

1. TIROS weather satellite: 525 miles (840 km)
2. Space Shuttle: 240 miles (385 km)
3. aurorae: 50 to 600 miles (80 to 960 km)
4. weather balloons: up to 23 miles (37 km)
5. highest manned balloon flight: 113,500 feet (35,050 m)
6. jet fighters: 60,000 feet (18,000 m)
7. jetliners: 40,000 feet (12,000 m)
8. Mt. Everest: 29,002 feet (8,848 m)
9. highest bird (bearded vulture): 25,000 feet (7,500 m)
10. mallard ducks: 21,000 feet (6,300 m)
11. helicopters: 10,000 feet (3,000 m)
12. Canada geese: 9,000 feet (2,700 m)

blackness of space. The particles of gas here are very hot during the daytime—perhaps 4,500° F (2,600° C)—but they are so few that they have no effect on any objects, such as spacecraft, that they hit.

Some areas of the country may be cracked by drought in summer (facing page), while others may be buried in snow just a few months later.

Catching Some Rays: Temperature

The sun radiates light and heat in all directions. The earth receives only 1/2,000,000,000 (one two-billionth) of the energy the sun produces. Much of the energy that hits the earth is reflected back into space. Most of the energy that isn't reflected is absorbed by the earth's surface—the ground, snow, or water. The surface warms, and in turn warms the air above it.

Just as the glass walls of a greenhouse trap sunlight, the very small amounts of water vapor and carbon dioxide in the air prevent some of the sun's heat from escaping into space. This is called *the greenhouse effect*, and it keeps the earth warm.

Temperature is a measure of the energy in the air. The more heat energy in the air, the higher the temperature.

The temperature of your area depends partially on what season it is. The earth tilts as it travels in its orbit around the sun. This causes the sun's rays to strike the earth at different angles.

On March 21, the spring equinox, sunlight falls directly on the equator. After June 21, the North Pole begins tipping gradually toward the sun. The northern half of the world, called the Northern Hemisphere, receives more direct sunlight. The days become longer, and it becomes summer there. The Southern Hemisphere receives less direct sunlight. Temperatures fall and it becomes autumn.

The Northern Hemisphere receives the most sunlight on June 21, the summer solstice. After June 21, the North Pole begins to tilt away from the sun. By September 23, the autumn equinox, sunlight is falling directly on the equator again. This date marks the beginning of fall in the Northern Hemisphere and the beginning of spring in the Southern Hemisphere.

As the North Pole keeps tipping away from the sun, the Southern Hemisphere warms. The Southern Hemisphere receives the most sun on December 22. Eventually the spring equinox returns on March 21, and the whole cycle starts over again.

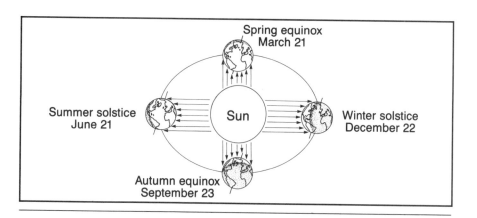

FEELING SAD

During the dim days of winter, some people feel unusually gloomy and sluggish. They suffer from SAD, or Seasonal Affective Disorder. Although the cause of SAD is unknown, there is a cure. Doctors have SAD patients spend time in the glow of panels that mimic natural sunlight. This treatment returns the patients to their sunny selves.

Feeling The Pressure

Air has more weight than you might think. At sea level, the air in a box three feet (one meter) on a side weighs about 2.6 pounds (1.2 kg). And there's a lot of air above you in the atmosphere. You never notice it, but the weight of all that air is continually pushing down on you, exerting about 15 pounds (6.8 kg) of pressure on every square inch of your body.

Meteorologists call the weight of the atmosphere over a certain point the *air pressure* or *barometric pressure*. The weight of the air above you is always changing, producing important turns in the weather.

Just Add Water

The air holds a lot of water. Think about the last time it rained and then the sun came out and it got hot. Did the air seem sticky or thick? That's because of water in the air. When liquid water is heated, it turns into water vapor, a gas. You've seen puddles on the sidewalk disappear for this reason. This process is called *evaporation*.

Water molecules are so small that 50 billion of them wouldn't fill a cup. And the hotter it gets, the more of them the air can hold:

• At 60° F (15° C), a cube of air one yard (meter) on each side can hold up to 4.48 ounces (125 g) of water (about a third of a soft drink can).

• At 104° F (40° C), the same cube of air can hold up to 17.9 ounces (500 g) of water (about 1½ soft drink cans). That's a lot of invisible water!

The amount of water vapor in the air is called the *humidity*. Meteorologists refer to the *relative humidity*, which is the amount of water in the air compared to how much the air can hold at the current temperature.

Say the relative humidity is 50%. That means that the air is currently holding half the water vapor that it is capable of

A home barometer for making predictions based on air pressure. A rising barometer often indicates clearing weather.

carrying. If the relative humidity is 100%, the air is holding all the water vapor it can, and no more evaporation can take place until the temperature goes up, or until the water vapor leaves the air. It does this through *condensation*, which is the opposite of evaporation. When water vapor condenses, it creates clouds.

Wind

Many weather changes are caused by temperature changes in the atmosphere. Heat mixes and moves air. Warm air expands and rises above cooler air. When a layer of air receives enough heat from the earth's surface, it moves upward. Colder air flows under it. The colder air is then warmed, and so it rises, too. The rising of warm air and sinking of cool air is called *convection*.

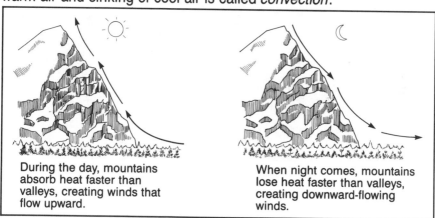

During the day, mountains absorb heat faster than valleys, creating winds that flow upward.

When night comes, mountains lose heat faster than valleys, creating downward-flowing winds.

Convection causes local breezes and winds. Different materials absorb and release different amounts of the sun's heat. Water, for instance, heats and cools more slowly than land, and cities heat more quickly than forests. Air rises over some areas and not over others, or it doesn't rise as quickly. This is what makes

Constant winds have sculpted these trees.

wind. Wind is simply a mass of air moving from one place
to another.

Convection also creates large weather patterns. The air near
the equator receives much more heat than the air near the earth's
poles. The warm air at the equator rises, and cold air from the poles
travels into warmer regions. Air constantly circulates around
the globe.

Highs and Lows

The unequal heating of the earth's surface means that different areas of air have different air pressures. These systems of air are called *high-* and *low-pressure systems*, or more simply *highs* and *lows*.

HIGHS

Highs usually bring fair weather. They often form in places where air cools, such as near the poles. As the air sinks, it slowly begins to turn. It moves clockwise in the Northern Hemisphere, and counterclockwise in the Southern Hemisphere. This rotating air is called an *anticyclone* or *high-pressure cell*. The air pressure increases closer to the center of the cell. In the Northern Hemisphere, pressure systems usually move from west to east.

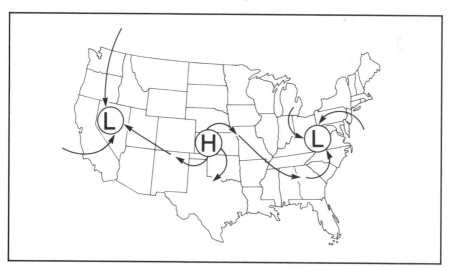

Lows

Low-pressure systems often bring cloudy, unsettled weather. They are created when air is heated, causing it to rise, expand, and cool. Lows rotate in a counterclockwise direction in the Northern Hemisphere, and in a clockwise direction in the Southern Hemisphere. Low-pressure cells are called *cyclones*.

Air always moves from areas of high pressure to areas of low pressure.

Pressure Point

Here's a fairly reliable rule (called Buys Ballot's Law) for finding highs and lows in the Northern Hemisphere: Stand with your back to the wind. The high pressure system is to your right and slightly behind you, and low pressure is to your left and slightly in front. (In the Southern Hemisphere, high pressure is to the left, and low to the right.)

In the Northern Hemisphere, a pressure system to your west might move over you. Remember that highs often bring fair weather, and that lows often bring foul weather.

Fronts

As you can guess, air over cold land or water tends to cool down. And air over warm surfaces warms up. It's no surprise that air over dry areas tends to stay dry. Over wet areas, air tends to get humid as it picks up water through evaporation.

HIGH

WIND

A key to weather forecasting is knowing about *air masses*. An air mass is a large body of air, often hundreds or thousands of miles across. All the air in an air mass has a similar temperature and humidity. For example, air masses move from Canada down into the United States. In the winter, Canada has low temperatures and low humidity. So the air masses that form there are cold and dry.

Storms are created when air masses meet each other. A *front* is the boundary between two air masses. Sometimes the differences between two air masses are hardly noticeable. But if colliding air masses have very different temperatures and amounts of water in them, turbulent weather can erupt.

A front is called a *cold front* when a cold air mass moves into the area occupied by a warmer air mass. The cold air is heavier, and so it forms a wedge that hugs the ground as it moves. Cold fronts bring lower temperatures and can create narrow bands of violent thunderstorms. In North America, cold fronts form on the eastern edges of high pressure systems. Cold fronts move at an average of about 20 mph (32 kph).

Clouds cover half the sky as a front moves in.

A front is called a *warm front* when a warm air mass moves into an area occupied by a colder air mass. The warm air is lighter, so it flows up the slope of the cold air below it.

Warm fronts usually form on the eastern sides of low pressure systems. They create wide areas of clouds and rain. Warm fronts do not move as quickly as cold fronts, averaging only about 15 mph (24 kph).

When a cold front follows and then overtakes a warm front, lifting the warmer air off the ground, an *occluded front* forms. Occluded fronts are combinations of both cold fronts and warm fronts.

High on this mountainside, cooling air forms clouds.

Clouds

As they move across the sky, clouds present an ever-changing spectacle. They're giant, beautiful banners, and their shapes and appearances can tell you a lot about what's happening in the atmosphere.

Clouds are formed in areas where air rises and cools. The

water vapor condenses, and small droplets of water form. These drops of water are very small—they're only about 1/2,500 of an inch (0.012 mm) across—but billions of them together form clouds that we can see.

Clouds can form:

• along warm and cold fronts, where warm air is forced upward over cold air

• near the tops of mountains, where air flows up the side of the mountain and cools as it rises higher into the atmosphere

• when warm air blows over a colder surface, such as a cool body of water

So if you see clouds growing, you know air above you is probably rising and cooling.

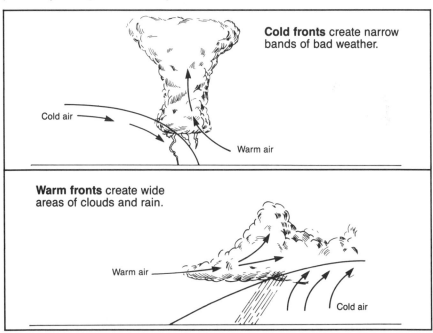

Cold fronts create narrow bands of bad weather.

Cold air

Warm air

Warm fronts create wide areas of clouds and rain.

Warm air

Cold air

INSTANT CLOUDS

You've made clouds before. In the wintertime, the air is cold. When you breathe in, air enters your lungs and is warmed. Your lungs also put a little water vapor into this warming air. When you exhale, your warm, moist breath hits the cold air, and the water vapor condenses almost immediately. This forms a mini-cloud that lasts for a second or two before it is blown apart.

Cloud Families

It's easy to recognize the different types of clouds. First, decide what the cloud's general shape is. If it looks like a sheet or layer, it's a *stratus cloud*, which means "layer." If it looks puffy, it's a *cumulus* cloud, which means "piled up."

Meteorologists divide these two general types of clouds into four more groups, which tell something about their height in the sky:

High clouds form above 20,000 feet (6,000 m). In this cold region of the troposphere, water almost always freezes, and clouds this high are usually made of tiny ice crystals. The main high clouds are the *cirrus, cirrocumulus,* and *cirrostratus.* They tend to be wispy, and are often transparent.

Clouds forming between 6,500 and 20,000 feet (1,950 and 6,000 m) are called **middle clouds**. They are made of water droplets. The major middle clouds are the *altostratus* and *altocumulus.*

Clouds found up to 6,500 feet (1,950 m) are **low clouds**. They include the *stratocumulus* and *nimbostratus* clouds. When *stratus* clouds lie on the ground, they are called *fog.*

Vertical clouds rise far above their bases and can form at many heights. *Cumulonimbus* clouds, or thunderheads, can start

You can often see several layers of clouds at the same time. These are cirrus clouds above a layer of fluffy cumulus clouds.

Fog is a cloud on the surface of the earth.

The streaky clouds of ice left behind by jets are called contrails.

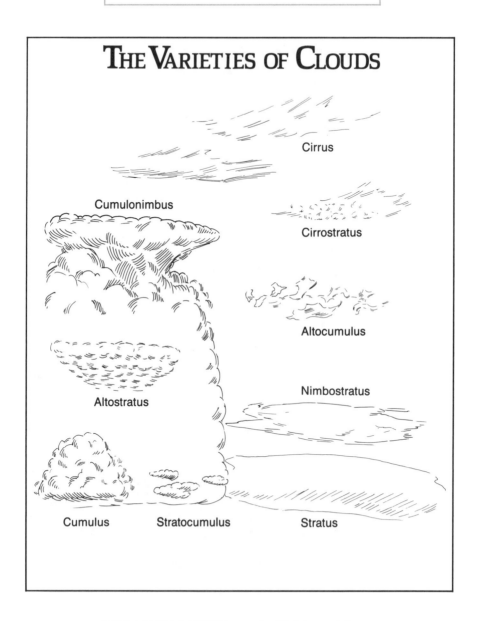

THE VARIETIES OF CLOUDS

Cirrus

Cumulonimbus

Cirrostratus

Altocumulus

Nimbostratus

Altostratus

Cumulus

Stratocumulus

Stratus

near the ground and soar up to 75,000 feet (22,500 m)! The fluffy *cumulus* is also a vertical cloud.

Along with these clouds, also watch for *contrails*. These are long white streaks of ice crystals which form behind jet planes in the upper troposphere and stratosphere. Contrails can disappear quickly, or may last for hours.

Your color cloud chart included with this kit features all major cloud types, plus some other interesting varieties. To identify the clouds you see in the sky, just match them with the clouds on your chart.

Recipes for Rain and Snow

This may surprise you, but clouds are always falling. The water droplets in them are being pulled down by gravity, but they fall at a very slow rate. Since they are so small and light, it may take them 21 days to fall just 1,000 feet. Wind currents can also lift cloud droplets easily. These are the reasons why clouds appear to float in the sky.

Some of the time, conditions are right for *precipitation*, which is moisture that falls out of clouds. It can take many forms. But it wasn't until the 1930s that meteorologists puzzled out how precipitation such as ordinary raindrops forms.

Liquid water falls as *rain* or *drizzle*. How do rain and drizzle drops form? All raindrops form around particles of salt or dust. Some of this dust comes from tiny meteorites and even the tails of comets. Water droplets stick to these particles. Then the drops attract more water and get bigger and bigger, until they are large enough to fall out of the cloud.

The quality of a snowball depends on the shape and size of snow crystals. Large, wet snowflakes are best.

In many clouds, raindrops actually begin as tiny ice crystals. These form when part or all of a cloud is below freezing. As the ice crystals fall inside the cloud, they may collide with water droplets, which freeze onto them. The ice crystals continue to grow larger. Eventually, they grow large enough to fall from the cloud. They pass through warm air, melt, and fall as raindrops.

Drizzle drops contain about one million cloud droplets. Raindrops are usually 1/10 to 1/4 inch (3 to 6 mm) across. Drizzle drops are 1/100 inch (.2 mm) across or smaller. Average-size raindrops contain more than 15 million cloud droplets! So you see, a raindrop has a lot of growing to do before it can fall.

When a cloud is very cold—between 10° and −4° F (−12° to −20° C)—*snow* may fall out of it. Snow is made of ice crystals. Water vapor freezes at these temperatures, forming ice crystals. As the ice crystals move within the cloud, many water droplets freeze onto them. This builds snow, which flutters out of the cloud. If the air is colder than 39° F (4° C), the flakes will land; otherwise, they melt. Most people think all snowflakes are six-pointed stars. Actually, most snowflakes are clumps of ice crystals shaped like columns, needles, spools, or clumps.

Acid Rain

Factories, power plants, refineries, and cars throw pollutants into the air. These chemicals mix with water and create acids. These acids rain down over wide areas, and are a serious threat to the environment. Acid rain has killed all the fish in thousands of lakes in Sweden, wiped out millions of trees in Germany, and has corroded the Statue of Liberty in New York City. New anti-pollution laws may reduce the amount of these chemicals in the air.

A *blizzard* is a powerful snowstorm that occurs when temperatures are below 20° F (−7° C) and the wind blows at 35 mph (56 kph) or more.

Acid rain has ruined this statue.

Luckily, hailstones as big as this don't fall from the sky very often!

Sleet is clear beads of ice. These beads were raindrops that froze as they fell through a layer of cold air.

Glaze is a coating of ice formed when raindrops freeze instantly upon hitting a cold surface. If glaze covers a large area, it is called an *ice storm*. Ice storms are dangerous because roads become slippery and power lines snap under the weight of the ice.

Hail is the largest form of precipitation. Hail forms in powerful thunderstorms. Strong wind currents carry water drops up into freezing sections of a cloud, where the water turns to ice. These nuggets of ice are then coated with water as they fall through the lower, warmer section of the cloud. Then they are tossed higher, where the water coating freezes. The hailstones are tossed up and

During an ice storm, rain cooled below 32° F hit this sprig of grass and froze instantly.

down inside the cloud, growing larger and heavier with each trip. When they grow too heavy, they fall all the way to the ground.

Hail is responsible for a great deal of damage to crops each year. Hailstones are usually about ½ inch (1 cm) across, but can be larger. The largest hailstone found in North America fell in Kansas on September 3, 1970. It weighed more than 1½ pounds (⅔ kg) and was 7½ inches (17½ cm) across!

IDENTICAL SNOWFLAKES?

People have always believed that no two snowflakes are the same. That is, until cloud scientist Nancy Knight spied these paired snowflakes on a plate of glass.

As it falls to the ground, a snowflake may pass through one million tiny changes in the temperature and humidity. These differences can lead to billions of different snowflake patterns.

Knight's column-shaped crystals are *very* much alike, but are probably not twins in every way. They may be similar because they

stuck to each other as they formed, encountering similar conditions as they fell.

The next time it snows, catch snowflakes on a piece of black paper or cloth, and look at them under a magnifying glass. Your chances of finding identical flakes are very, very slim—but the variety and complexity of your snowflakes will amaze you.

Dew

If you notice the ground is wet when you get up in the morning, it doesn't mean that it rained during the night. This water might be *dew*. Dew is not precipitation. It is water that forms on surfaces that have cooled below the condensation temperature, or

Tiny drops of dew form on a spiderweb.

Feathery frost on a windowpane.

dewpoint, of the air. You can find dew on grass, spider webs, and cars, especially after cool, clear nights.

The "sweat" that forms on the outside of a drinking glass is dew, too. The cold glass cools the air around it to the point where water vapor condenses.

Like dew, *frost* also forms on cold surfaces. But frost forms when the surface temperature is below freezing. At these times, water vapor in the air turns directly into ice, which can form beautiful designs on windowpanes and other smooth surfaces.

WEATHER CONTROL

Under certain conditions, it may be possible to influence the weather. A controversial technique known as *cloud seeding* may encourage clouds to produce rain or snow. Using airplanes, rockets, or blowers on the ground, meteorologists scatter tiny crystals of a chemical called silver iodide into the air. Ice crystals then grow around the silver iodide until they fall from the cloud as snow or rain.

Cloud seeding is rarely performed, and seems to work only when conditions are almost right for natural precipitation.

PART TWO

Wild
Weather

When the conditions are right, nature can produce incredible displays of beauty and power. Violent storms are unpredictable. Watching their growth and movement is a top concern of meteorologists, because lives and property are often at stake. Here are the secrets of Earth's wildest weather.

Thunder and Lightning

A cold wind gusts against your face, blowing your hair around. To the west, you see angry black clouds towering miles into the air. The air smells crisp, and you can hear the low rumble of thunder as the clouds draw nearer. You know it's time to head indoors—a bad summer thunderstorm is on its way.

Thunderstorms are cumulonimbus clouds. These large clouds hold a great deal of water droplets. Warm updrafts, or convection currents, inside the cloud lift the water droplets, making the cloud taller. As the water rises, it cools rapidly, and rain begins to fall.

During these storms, static electricity builds up within the clouds. You've seen and felt static electricity in your home. Sometimes when you walk across a carpet in your sneakers, you build up static electricity in your body. Then when you touch another person or a metal object, a spark jumps from your finger, maybe even making a "zap" sound.

Lightning bolts are giant sparks of static electricity. A positive charge builds in the upper part of the cloud. A large negative charge builds in the lower portion. When the difference between the positive and negative charges becomes great, the electrical charge jumps from one area to another, creating a lightning bolt.

Most lightning bolts strike from one cloud to another, but the most dramatic and dangerous ones are those that strike the ground. These bolts occur when positive charges build up on the ground.

A lightning bolt can heat the air hotter than the surface of the sun.

A negative charge called the *leader* flows from the cloud toward the ground. Then a positively-charged leader leaves the ground and runs into the cloud. This is called the *return stroke*. What you see as a lightning bolt is actually a series of downward-striking leaders and upward-striking return strokes, all taking place in less than a second! The strokes and returns happen so quickly that your eyes see them as one bolt.

These bolts can heat the air to 30,000°—hotter than the surface of the sun. This burst of heat makes the air around the bolt expand explosively, producing the sound we hear as thunder. Since light travels a million times faster than sound, we see lightning bolts before we hear their thunderclaps.

It's easy to estimate how far away you are from a lightning bolt. Just count the number of seconds between the time you see the lightning flash and the time you hear the thunder. Since sound travels about one mile in five seconds, just divide the number of seconds you counted by five. The result tells you how many miles away the lightning is.

There's an old saying that lightning never strikes the same place twice. Don't believe it! Leaders are attracted to tall objects such as mountaintops and buildings. The Empire State Building, for instance, is hit an average of 23 times a year.

Here are more unusual facts about thunderstorms:

• There are 2,000 thunderstorms in progress around the world at any given moment.

• Each year, there are 100 million lightning discharges in the United States.

• Lightning bolts can be very long, often stretching 100 miles.

• Lightning kills about 100 people and starts more than 10,000 fires in the United States each year.

LIGHTNING SAFETY

When a thunderstorm threatens, take shelter in the ground floor of a building. If you are outside, stay away from trees, flagpoles, or hilltops, because lightning is attracted to tall objects. If you're swimming, leave the beach or the swimming pool. One of the safest places to be is inside a car, because the metal body spreads the bolt and directs it into the ground.

Tall buildings are usually protected by *lightning rods*. Invented by Benjamin Franklin, these metal rods channel the electricity from lightning bolts into the ground, where it does no harm.

Tornadoes

They are the most unpredictable of weather events. Although they can't twirl away houses as one did in *The Wizard of Oz*, tornadoes are powerful and often deadly.

Tornadoes are created in powerful thunderstorms. As a column of warm air rises, air rushes in at ground level and begins to spin. If the storm gathers energy, a twisting, spinning funnel develops. In many cases, the funnel doesn't reach the earth. But in the most energetic storms, the tornado funnel descends to the ground.

In these tornadoes, the roaring winds in the funnel can reach more than 300 mph (480 kph)—the strongest winds on earth. Funnels usually travel at 20 to 40 mph (32 to 64 kph), moving toward the northeast. Tornadoes will occasionally form over lakes or oceans. These suck water into the funnel cloud and are called *waterspouts*.

Tornadoes travel short distances, usually less than 10 miles (16 km), and often hop and skip over the countryside, touching down, lifting, and then touching down again. The bases of tornadoes are usually about 700 feet (200 meters) across. The most terrible twisters have been monsters, with paths a mile wide and dozens of miles long.

The funnels destroy everything they touch. As they hit houses, their winds push the nearest wall inward and lift the roof, blowing the other walls outward. Objects sucked into funnels can be ejected with great force, turning them into deadly missiles. Tornadoes can

The strongest winds on earth are tornadoes.

drive pieces of straw into trees as if they were nails, and they have lifted freight trains from their tracks.

The Great Plains of the United States is called "Tornado Alley." This area is the world's greatest tornado factory. The United States experiences about 770 tornadoes each year. Large thunderstorm systems can generate groups of twisters called *outbreaks*. The famous Superoutbreak of April 3–4, 1974, twirled out 148 tornadoes! They caused $600,000,000 in damage and killed 315 people in the midwestern United States.

A tornado in Indiana caused this damage.

The British expression, "It's raining cats, dogs, and pitchforks" is illustrated in this cartoon.

The latest weather radars are especially useful for spotting thunderstorms that create tornadoes, and meteorologists are usually able to give people advance warning. The National Weather Service issues a *tornado watch* when conditions are suitable for tornado formation, and a *tornado warning* when a tornado has been spotted in the air or touching the ground.

A hurricane spins into the gulf of Mexico.

Wacky Winds

In the United States, tornadoes have sucked frogs from ponds and marshes and into the air, causing rains of frogs over populated areas. In England, waterspouts or violent updrafts probably caused the rain of flounder reported in east London in 1984, the shower of starfish and periwinkles seen in Yorkshire in 1984, and the brief but heavy rain of frogs in Wiltshire in 1939.

There is no record anywhere of a rain of cats and dogs.

Hurricanes

While tornadoes are less than a mile wide, hurricanes can blow paths of destruction 400 miles (650 km) across. Fortunately, they take days or weeks to form—enough time to prepare for them.

Hurricanes begin near the equator, usually in the late spring and summer. In their earliest stages, they are called *tropical cyclones* and are nothing more than simple low-pressure systems. Hot, moist air begins spinning in the normal cyclone way—counterclockwise in the Northern Hemisphere, and clockwise in the Southern Hemisphere. But unlike storms over land, the warm ocean provides the developing tropical storm with a continuous source of heat energy.

"Hurricane hunters" fly into the eye of the storm to record data.

If a tropical cyclone continues to grow in power and its winds reach 38 mph (60 kph), it is then classified as a *tropical depression*. Its winds begin circulating faster, and the storm system may begin traveling across the ocean at up to 15 mph (24 kph).

Meteorologists carefully watch depressions for signs of growth. One in ten depressions will grow into a *tropical storm*, where the winds may reach 73 mph (117 kph). Tropical storms can dump huge amounts of rain.

A tropical storm may gather strength and become a full-blown hurricane. (These storms are called *typhoons* in the Pacific Ocean and *willy-willies* in Australia.) They may move as fast as 50 mph (80 kph), with winds of at least 74 mph (118 kph), and perhaps as high as 150 mph (240 kph).

From space, hurricanes look like giant pinwheels. Their winds circulate around an *eye*, or center, between 5 and 25 miles (8 and 40 km) across. Although the areas around the eye of a hurricane are violently windy and rainy, the eye itself is strangely calm. The winds there are light, and the sky is often clear. People sometimes go out into the eye, thinking that the hurricane has passed, only to be hit by the hurricane's other side.

Hurricanes are incredibly destructive when they hit land. The high winds uproot trees, tear down power lines, and destroy buildings. The strongest hurricanes may create tornadoes. Hurricanes also cause high waves and tides up to 25 feet (7.5 m) above normal, which wash away buildings along beaches. These waves and the heavy flooding they bring are the greatest cause of hurricane deaths. Fortunately, hurricanes lose power rapidly as soon as they leave the ocean.

The Atlantic Ocean experiences an average of six hurricanes a year. Hurricanes can be tracked with radar and satellites, but they can be unpredictable and it's often difficult to guess exactly where they will strike the coast.

The National Weather Service updates the progress of tropical storms four times a day. It issues a *hurricane watch* when there is a threat of hurricane conditions within 24 to 36 hours, and issues a *hurricane warning* when hurricane conditions are expected in a specific area.

NAMING HURRICANES

Every tropical storm receives a name for easy reference and identification. The names repeat every six years. Here are the names of Atlantic Ocean storms for 1991 through 1996:

1991	1992	1993	1994	1995	1996
Ana	Andrew	Arlene	Alberto	Allison	Arthur
Bob	Bonnie	Bret	Beryl	Barry	Bertha
Claudette	Charley	Cindy	Chris	Chantal	Cesar
Danny	Danielle	Dennis	Debby	Dean	Diana
Erika	Earl	Emily	Ernesto	Erin	Edouard
Fabian	Frances	Floyd	Florence	Felix	Fran
Grace	Georges	Gert	Gordon	Gabrielle	Gustav
Henri	Hermine	Harvey	Helene	Hugo	Hortense
Isabel	Ivan	Irene	Isaac	Iris	Isidore
Juan	Jeanne	Jose	Joyce	Jerry	Josephine
Kate	Karl	Katrina	Keith	Karen	Klaus
Larry	Lisa	Lenny	Leslie	Luis	Lili
Mindy	Mitch	Maria	Michael	Marilyn	Marco
Nicholas	Nicole	Nate	Nadine	Noel	Nana
Odette	Otto	Ophelia	Oscar	Opal	Omar
Peter	Paula	Philippe	Patty	Pablo	Paloma
Rose	Richard	Rita	Rafael	Roxanne	Rene
Sam	Shary	Stan	Sandy	Sebastien	Sally
Teresa	Tomas	Tammy	Tony	Tanya	Teddy
Victor	Virginie	Vince	Valerie	Van	Vicky
Wanda	Walter	Wilma	William	Wendy	Wilfred

Special Effects

When weather conditions are right, sunlight can create unusual displays in the sky. You'll be able to spot these effects if you look regularly. But be careful never to look directly into the sun!

It's possible to see *rainbows* when you are between the sun and a rain shower. Light rays from the sun enter falling raindrops, bounce around inside them, and then exit the drops. The drops separate sunlight into different colors, which appear as giant curved bands in the sky. Sometimes a smaller rainbow will form underneath the main bow. You can create artificial rainbows by creating a fine spray of water with a garden hose.

Since the light bouncing from the raindrops scatters in many directions, observers on the ground see the same rainbow in slightly different ways. No two people can see the exact same rainbow.

Halos around the sun and moon are created when light passes through the ice crystals of cirrus clouds. The most common is the "small" halo. Ice crystals in the clouds bend and refract the light into bright circles around the sun and moon. Halos often signal the approach of bad weather. Sometimes halos feature brighter spots of light. These are called *sundogs*.

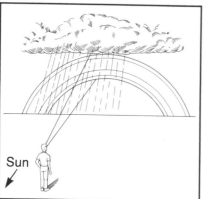

Sun

When the sun is low, ice crystals can produce *light pillars*. These are columns of light that extend above and sometimes below the sun itself. *Crepuscular rays* are beautiful effects that look like lances or fingers of sunlight. They are created when dust particles or clouds partially block the sun. You can see them frequently.

An assortment of special effects. This page: halo (top) and crepuscular rays.
Facing page: sun dog (left) and sun pillar.

PART THREE

Tracking the Weather

Now that you know the basic causes of changes in the weather, you're ready to become an amateur meteorologist. By using some of the same rules that professional meteorologists rely on, you'll be able to make accurate forecasts of the weather in your area.

The Professionals

Meteorology is a young science. Although the first weather map of the United States was drawn in 1831, scientists didn't understand the movement of air masses until 1918. But meteorological science has developed rapidly. People interested in becoming meteorologists go to college and take math, physics, and meteorology classes. They learn about the instruments and techniques that can help them look into the future.

The easiest way to know what the weather will be like tomorrow is to know what the weather is like in the areas around you. This gives you a general picture of what's happening in the atmosphere and lets you know what weather patterns are moving toward you. This is called *synoptic* (sin-OP-tik) *forecasting*.

This information is provided by the National Weather Service, which is operated by the federal government. It collects weather observations from around the world and issues official weather forecasts. The National Weather Service operates 550 observation stations in the United States. Data about temperature, wind speed, humidity, and so forth are collected from these stations several times a day. The Weather Service also receives reports from other countries. Meteorologists can then see where the weather is changing anywhere in the world.

Meteorologists also use other tools. Weather balloons carry transmitters called *radiosondes* high into the atmosphere. These devices transmit information on temperature, air pressure, humidity, and wind back to the ground.

Weather scientists at work on Ellesmere Island, Canada

Weather radars send radio waves through the air to detect precipitation. The newest, called *Doppler radars*, can also measure the speed and direction of rain and ice. These radars make it possible to detect the motions in the air that lead to tornadoes. This allows meteorologists time to issue tornado warnings.

The National Weather Service also operates weather satellites. Some orbit the earth about every 100 minutes, and others always hang above the same spot on the earth. With their television cameras, weather satellites transmit pictures showing the movement of clouds and air masses. Satellites can also measure temperature and humidity from space. They are especially useful for tracking storms and watching the development of hurricanes.

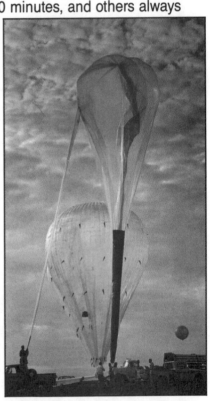

The National Weather Service shares its information with whoever needs it. The United States and other countries exchange weather observations through the World Meteorological Organization of the United Nations. The meteorologists at your local television and radio stations also receive National Weather Service information. They use it along with their own observations and knowledge to make forecasts for your area.

Balloons launched by the National Center for Atmospheric Research gather information about air temperature, humidity, and pressure.

You can get National Weather Service information from the National Oceanic and Atmospheric Administration (NOAA). NOAA provides taped weather messages from its 350 offices. Your phone book has the number of the nearest office. NOAA also operates a network of weather radio stations. These broadcast current conditions and forecasts 24 hours a day on FM frequencies between 162.40 and 162.55 megahertz (MHz). Most household radios do not pick up these signals, but you can buy weather radios that do.

The government also offers information through the mail. A useful and interesting publication is the Daily Weather Map series. This publication features detailed weather maps for the past week. You can order them by writing to:

> Daily Weather Maps
> Climate Analysis Center, Room 808
> World Weather Building
> Washington, D.C. 20233

Daily Weather Maps cost $1.50 each. You should pay with a check or money order made out to the Department of Commerce, NOAA.

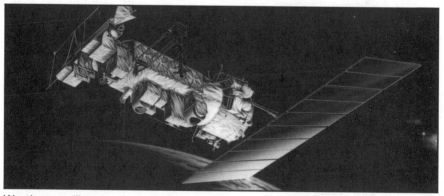

Weather satellites can help pinpoint forest fires, record ocean temperatures, and warn of storms.

Setting Up Your Weather Station

Making observations is essential for forecasting. The weather station included in this kit can provide you with the temperature, wind direction, wind speed, the amount of rainfall, and the wind chill factor.

You'll need a screwdriver to install your weather station. You might also ask an adult to assist you. Follow these steps:

1. Set up your weather station outdoors, away from buildings, trees, and other objects that may block wind and rain. The ideal base for your weather station is a post or fence.

2. Mount the swivel (A) to your base with the screws (B). Make sure the swivel is straight up and down and not tilted.

3. Slide the direction rose (C) over the swivel. Position the rose so it points north.

4. Snap the wind speed indicator (D) onto the body of the station (E).

5. Slide the body of the station onto the swivel and secure it with the cap (F). Make sure it swings freely.

6. To keep your weather station in perfect working condition, clean it from time to time with a damp cloth. Wash the rain gauge with soap and water.

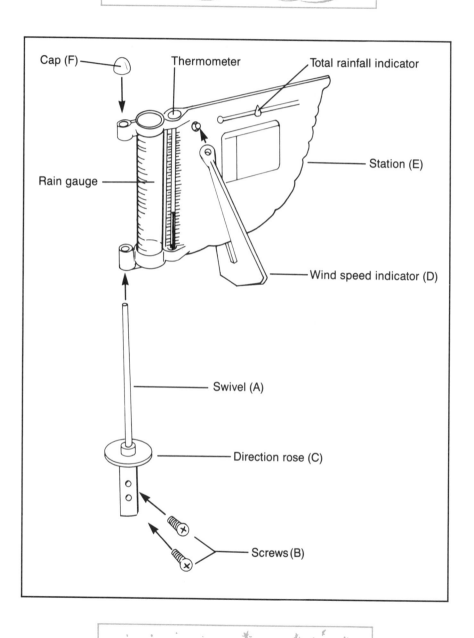

Cap (F)

Thermometer

Total rainfall indicator

Station (E)

Rain gauge

Wind speed indicator (D)

Swivel (A)

Direction rose (C)

Screws (B)

Keeping Your Weather Log

The first step in forecasting is gathering and recording data with your weather station. It's best to take measurements at least twice a day. It is important to make your observations *at the same time each day*. By keeping consistent records, you'll be able to compare conditions from month to month and from year to year.

Record the following information on the weather log that begins on page 78:

TEMPERATURE

The thermometer in your weather station tells you the temperature in degrees Fahrenheit and degrees Celsius. The National Weather Service and most newspapers, television stations, and radio stations in the United States use the Fahrenheit scale. Most foreign countries use Celsius. You can record one or both.

WIND DIRECTION AND SPEED

When a weather report says that winds are southerly, then the wind is blowing from the south. Using the direction rose at the base of your station, record the direction from which the wind blows.

The wind will cause the wind speed indicator to rise. Record the wind speed by reading the average number the arm points to as you watch it for a minute or two. If the wind speed is rising and

A meteorologist at the National Weather Service

Weather vanes have been used for hundreds of years to show the direction of the wind.

falling rapidly, the wind is *gusty*. Record the average speed and the top speed of the gusts.

You can record the wind speed in miles per hour. If you live near a lake or the sea, you may want to use the *Beaufort Wind Scale*, which is named after the British admiral who invented it in 1805. Sailing winds are measured in *knots* (one knot is a little more than one mile per hour, or about 1.7 kph). The Beaufort Scale also allows you to estimate speeds by how the wind affects objects:

Beaufort Wind Scale

MPH	KPH	KNOTS	BEAUFORT NUMBER	DESCRIPTION	EFFECTS
0–1	0–2	0–1	0	calm	smoke rises straight up; water like mirror
1–3	2–5	1–3	1	light air	smoke drifts slowly; ripples on water
4–7	5–11	4–6	2	slight breeze	leaves rustle; small wavelets
8–12	11–19	7–10	3	gentle breeze	leaves and twigs in motion; large wavelets, scattered whitecaps up to 1½ feet tall
13–18	19–29	11–16	4	moderate breeze	small branches move, loose paper blows; small waves 2 to 4 feet tall
19–24	29–38	17–21	5	fresh breeze	small trees sway; many whitecaps 4–8 feet tall, some spray
25–31	38–50	22–27	6	strong breeze	large branches sway, telephone wires whistle; whitecaps everywhere with waves 8–13 feet tall
32–38	50–60	28–33	7	near gale	whole trees in motion, becomes hard to walk against wind; waves 13 feet tall, foam from waves begins to blow
39–46	60–74	34–40	8	gale	twigs break off trees; waves up to 16 feet tall
47–54	74–86	41–47	9	strong gale	branches break, minor damage to houses; high, rolling waves up to 21 feet, damage to beaches
55–63	86–101	48–55	10	whole gale	trees blown over (seldom seen inland); overhanging crests on waves up to 26 feet tall; sea is white
64–73	101–117	56–63	11	storm	widespread damage; exceptionally high waves up to 35 feet tall
74–up	117–up	64–up	12	hurricane	widespread damage; air filled with foam, large ships sink

WIND CHILL

On cool days, the wind sucks heat away from your body, making the temperature feel much lower than your thermometer says it is. This effect is called the *wind chill*. This chart tells you how cold it really feels:

WIND SPEED (mph)	WIND CHILL (°F)											
	45	40	35	30	25	20	15	10	5	0	−5	−10
4	45	40	35	30	25	20	15	10	5	0	−5	−10
5	43	37	32	27	22	16	11	6	0	−5	−10	−15
10	34	26	22	16	10	3	−3	−9	−15	−22	−27	−34
15	29	23	16	9	2	−5	−11	−18	−25	−31	−38	−45
20	26	19	12	4	−3	−10	−17	−24	−31	−39	−46	−53
25	23	16	8	1	−7	−15	−22	−29	−36	−44	−51	−59
30	21	13	6	−2	−10	−18	−25	−33	−41	−49	−56	−64
35	20	12	4	−4	−12	−20	−27	−35	−43	−52	−58	−67
40	19	11	3	−5	−13	−21	−29	−37	−45	−53	−60	−69
45	18	10	2	−6	−14	−22	−30	−38	−46	−54	−62	−70

Your weather station includes a shorter version of this chart for quick reference.

These unusual cloud formations, called lenticular clouds, are often mistaken for flying saucers.

VISIBILITY

The atmosphere contains a tremendous number of dust particles. The more particles in the air, the harder it is to see distant objects.

If you know how far away local landmarks are, you can record the number of miles or kilometers you can see. If you can see to the horizon, visibility is unlimited.

Sky Coverage

How much of the sky is covered by clouds? Make your best guess, and then record it using these symbols:

○	No clouds	◐	Six-tenths covered
⊙	One-tenth covered	◕	Seven to eight-tenths covered
◔	Two to three-tenths covered	◖	Nine-tenths covered
◔	Four-tenths covered	●	Completely overcast
◑	Half covered	⊗	Sky obscured

Cloud Types

Use your cloud chart to decide what kinds of clouds you see. There may be a mix of types. You can record your observations by writing the scientific names of the clouds, or by using these symbols:

LOW CLOUDS	⌒	Cumulus
	△	Cumulus (vertical)
	⌣	Stratocumulus
	—	Stratus
	⌂	Cumulonimbus

MIDDLE CLOUDS	∠	Altostratus
	⦫	Nimbostratus
	∽	Altocumulus

HIGH CLOUDS	⌐	Cirrus
	∠	Cirrostratus
	∠⌐	Cirrostratus (covering entire sky)
	⌒	Cirrocumulus

CURRENT WEATHER

Use this space to record the important weather events you see. Use as many of these symbols as you need:

	Slight	Steady	Intermittent/ Moderate	Steady/ Moderate	Intermittent/ Heavy	Steady/ Heavy
DRIZZLE						
RAIN						
SNOW						

69

Ice pellets	⏴⬤⏵	Freezing drizzle	⌣⌣
Hail	⬦	Blowing dust	S→
Freezing rain	⌢•	Fog	≡
Haze	∞	Thunderstorm	⎰
Smoke	⌢⌣	Snow shower	*▽
Light fog	=	Thunderstorm and rain	⬤⎰
Tornado	)(	Hurricane	⟲

PRECIPITATION

Use the rain gauge on your weather station to find out how many inches of rain fall during a shower. Empty the rain gauge at the end of each day to determine the daily rainfall.

You should note how heavy the rainfall is, too. Rainfall is *light* if your gauge gets less than 1/10 of an inch (25 mm) per hour. Rainfall is *moderate* if you collect 1/10 to 3/10 of an inch (25 mm to 75 mm) per hour; it is *heavy* if more than 3/10 of an inch (75 mm) falls per hour.

If it snows, measure its depth with a ruler. Pick a spot that represents the average depth, not a place where the snow has

blown into a drift. Ten inches of snow usually equals about one inch of rain. You can also melt the snow that collects in your rain gauge to see how much rain it equals.

AIR PRESSURE

Meteorologists use instruments called *barometers* to record the air pressure.

If you have a barometer, record the air pressure and note if it is rising or falling. You can also get accurate air pressure readings from television and radio reports.

Clouds are clues to changes in the weather. These cumulonimbus clouds threaten rain.

NOTES

Use this space to note anything interesting you observe: rainbows, halos, the size of hailstones, how long a rainfall lasts, how far away lightning is, and so on. Pay attention to how long after you see a halo it rains or snows.

	Date: 5/27 Time: 9am	Date: 5/27 Time: 1pm	Date: 5/27 Time: 5pm	Date: 5/28 Time: 9am
Temperature:	68°F	73°F	64°F	65°F
Wind speed:	6 mph	10-15 mph	15-20 mph	5 mph
Wind direction:	S to SE	S	SW	W
Wind chill:	—	—	60°	→
Visibility:	good	good	¼ mile (rain)	excellent
Sky coverage:	◗	◖	●	◑
Cloud types:	⊍	⊠	⊠ R	→
Current weather:				sunny
Precipitation:	none	none	⋮	none
Air pressure:	30.01 ↓	29.95 ↓	29.90	30.21 steady
Notes:	altocumulous clouds and falling pressure.	air pressure falling rapidly	hail ½ inch across	1 inch of rain last night.
Predictions:	storm approaching. clearing in 24 hours			good weather for next few days

Here's a sample page from a weather log, showing changes over 24 hours. Your weather log begins on page 78.

In the desert, hot air rises and creates a low-pressure funnel that sucks up dirt. The resulting mini-tornado is called a dust devil.

Making Forecasts

Forecasting allows you to put your observations to work. Predicting weather is not an exact science. Professional meteorologists are sometimes surprised by unexpected weather changes. Don't be discouraged if your predictions are off—a little practice and good record-keeping will improve your accuracy.

FORECASTING WITH MAPS

The most common and useful weather information comes from weather maps. You can find a basic map in your newspaper. It shows major high- and low-pressure systems, temperatures, fronts, and areas of precipitation. The edges of cold fronts are marked with spiked lines; warm fronts are marked with bumpy lines. Newspaper weather maps will help you make accurate predictions up to 24 hours in advance.

Save each day's map, and write its date on top. As you save maps, you'll notice:

- the direction that fronts and weather patterns are moving
- how fast the fronts are moving
- what temperatures and weather are being recorded in front of and behind the fronts

With this information, you can guess where the fronts will move next, and how long it will take them to arrive.

ANIMAL FORECASTERS

Over the centuries, people have relied on animals to help them forecast the weather. Some methods work, and some don't.

- Crickets are reliable, living thermometers. Count how many times a cricket chirps in 15 seconds, then add 37. The result is the temperature in degrees Fahrenheit.

- Birds don't like to fly before storms. They can detect the low pressure that often signals the arrival of bad weather. Here's an old saying about robins:

> If the robin sings in the bush
> Then the weather will be coarse;
> If the robin sings on the barn
> Then the weather will be warm.

If you listen closely, crickets can tell you the temperature!

• According to tradition, if the groundhog sees its shadow on February 2, winter will last for six more weeks. And if it's cloudy when the groundhog appears, spring will come early. Weatherwise, there is nothing special about February 2 or groundhogs.

• Farmers often say that if cows lie down, then a storm is coming. But cows also lie down in good weather. It doesn't necessarily have something to do with the weather. Maybe it just means the cows are tired.

FORECASTING BY CLOUD TYPES

Your cloud chart tells you the weather that different types of clouds bring. By looking at your weather log, you can also see what types of clouds have moved into your area over the past day. With practice, you'll soon recognize the weather changes that accompany new cloud formations.

They may look trustworthy, but don't rely on groundhogs to predict the weather.

FORECASTING BY HIGHS AND LOWS

Air pressure and wind direction can tell you about the air masses moving into your area. Get the barometer reading from the newspaper, television, or radio. Then find out from which direction the wind is blowing:

BAROMETER (at sea level)	WIND DIRECTION	FORECAST
30.01 to 30.20 steady	SW to NW	fair for 1 to 2 days
30.01 to 30.20 rising rapidly	SW to NW	fair, followed by rain within 2 days
30.20 and above steady	SW to NW	continued fair
30.20 and above slowly falling	SW to NW	fair for 2 days, slowly rising temperatures
30.10 to 30.20 falling slowly	S to SE	rain within 24 hours
30.10 to 30.20 falling	S to SE	rain in 12 to 24 hours
30.10 to 30.20 falling rapidly	SE to NE	rain within 12 hours
30.10 and above falling slowly	E to NE	in summer, usually no precipitation, in winter, precipitation within 24 hours
30.10 and above falling rapidly	E to NE	good chance of precipitation within 24 hours
30.00 or below falling slowly	SE to NE	rain continuing for 1 to 2 days
30.00 or below falling rapidly	SE to NE	rain and wind, clearing within 24 hours
30.10 or below rising slowly	S to SW	clearing soon with fair weather to come
29.80 or below falling rapidly	S to E	severe storms approaching, clearing after 24 hours
29.80 or below falling rapidly	E to N	severe storms with heavy precipitation

These are only general rules. Remember that many forces affect the weather. Keep an eye on the sky, and you'll always be rewarded.

	Date: Time:	Date: Time:	Date: Time:	Date: Time:
Temperature:				
Wind speed:				
Wind direction:				
Wind chill:				
Visibility:				
Sky coverage:				
Cloud types:				
Current weather:				
Precipitation:				
Air pressure:				
Notes:				
Predictions:				

	Date: Time:	Date: Time:	Date: Time:	Date: Time:
Temperature:				
Wind speed:				
Wind direction:				
Wind chill:				
Visibility:				
Sky coverage:				
Cloud types:				
Current weather:				
Precipitation:				
Air pressure:				
Notes:				
Predictions:				

	Date: Time:	Date: Time:	Date: Time:	Date: Time:
Temperature:				
Wind speed:				
Wind direction:				
Wind chill:				
Visibility:				
Sky coverage:				
Cloud types:				
Current weather:				
Precipitation:				
Air pressure:				
Notes:				
Predictions:				